Frail Bird

Words On A Wing

DAVID SANFORD RIDGWAY

Copyright © 2020 by David Sanford Ridgway.

ISBN   Softcover   978-1-950596-87-4

All rights reserved. No part of this book may be reproduced or transmitted in any form or by any means, electronic or mechanical, including photocopying, recording, or by any information storage and retrieval system without express written permission from the author, except in the case of brief quotations embodied in critical reviews and certain other non-commercial uses permitted by copyright law.

Printed in the United States of America.

To order additional copies of this book, contact:
Bookwhip
1-855-339-3589
www.bookwhip.com

Contents

The Music of Waves 7
Father 8
Infinity 10
Frail Bird 11
Black and White 12
Rembrandt's Ruins 13
Speaking in Tongues 14
Street Search 15
Shades of Blue 17
Storm 18
Word Play 19
Lost and Found 20
Crawling 21
Spiritual Songs 22
Love Embers 23
Sun and Shadows 24
Lost Lives 25
Out of the Shadows 26
Rain 27
A Thin Wall 28
Words 29
Riding the Wave 30
Love Twice 31
Change 32
Storyteller 33

Sanctuary..34
Starting Over...36
First Love 38
Boy at the Beach... 40
One Word 41
Love Embers 42
No Words 43
Begin 44
Rain 45
Bright Beings 46
Lost and Found 47
Soul Searching.. 48
Tunnel..49
Sea of Doubt... 50

The Music of Waves

The sea sings
a song of
love and nature
nurturing me

with its rumbling
power humbling
me as I
walk in awe

of the spiritual
peace and amazing
love that the
ocean gives us

and we need
to love it
back and not
destroy its

soulful serenity
with the poison
of pollution we
spew out every

day and clean
the ocean as
it clears our
souls forever

Father

Alone at a
table listening
to my father
lecturing about

business and
what I should
do with my
life losing

weight working
never once
congratulating
me on recovery

walking on my
knee living
on my own
living in my

bipolar world
taking care
of my own
life but my

father is all
about himself
and being in
control of

everyone and
giving love
with many
conditions never

reaching out
and touching
my love and
it must be lonely
in his world

Infinity

The wind screams
and we are anxious
the gray sky
turns us melancholy

but the sun's glow
widens our smiles
and the moonbeams
calm our fears

the steady rain
turns to sorrow
the storm feeds
our angry words

but the sunshine
warms our hearts
and we sail
on to infinity

Frail Bird

Frail and flapping
its weak wings
trying to fly
away from the

black storm and
the rain comes
in torrents but
the wispy wings

grow stronger
and the bird's
long flight finds
sunlight streaming

in my window
washing away my
trail of tears
smiling at my

pools of pain
and the frail
bird and I
fly on

Black and White

I walk
down a black
road surrounded
by dark forces

Demons chasing
my lonely soul
I search in
vain for sun

wanting to
wallow in a
white sea
I am struck

by the two
poles resting
between black
and white

standing on
the ledge
gray ghosts
looking for

salvation I
try to exist
between black
and bright white

Rembrandt's Ruins

Young boy plays
with a jar
of paint making
colors outside the

lines that no one
can see experimenting
shadows sunlight
inhabiting the world

of pompous priests
critical renaissance never ends
the man Rembrandt
painting his soul

till death comes
still searching longingly
light lurking in
on Rembrandt ruins

Speaking in Tongues

Words winding
down
a path
pebbles

in my
shoes
writing words
language

speaking in
tongues
speeches that
no one

will
ever hear
translating
into

the storm that
rages in my
mind you are
my rock steady

forever as we
wait for our
bodies to join
hearts beat as one

Street Search

She walks
the
streets searching
for

a fix
wanting to
sail
away getting

away
from pain
putting
the needle
in

her arm
she
thinks she
is

free but
sweet
slavery holds
like

a prison
cell
dying a

little
bit at
a
time

lying on
the
dirty ground
death

all around
Satan
takes her
soul

Shades of Blue

Dark blue
curtain of
desolation seeing
only sadness

Royal blue
open your
eyes go
toward awakening

Teal proclaiming
salvation good
thoughts smiles
replacing frowns

The light is
blue we
walk a road
to God.

Storm

Rumbling rain taps out
its maudlin melody God
is lost in the
storm and our sons
and daughters search
in vain for his
sun smiling

Word Play

Bouncing bubbling
feelings
fire burning
out

I look
at
writings word
play

picking pieces
scattered
across
sandy beaches

bound
together with
string
sunshine smiles

Lost and Found

If
we go
down the street
slicing our feet on

broken glass it takes
ghost haunting our
lonely souls
going

Into
the lost
and found yelling
to hear ourselves think

The wheels are winding
in our heads
silent angels
frost bitten

Crawling

Crawling through
the boneyards
of broken
hearts howling

last gasps
dying days
look to
the Great

spirit lifting
light from
burning shores
water wings

ancient air
blowing breaths
walking winds
naked night

Spiritual Songs

Music meanders like
waves washing over
hearts hurting calming
our angry minds

Singing spiritual songs
the words wander
different tunes but
common love lyrics

We all need
voices from the
past comforting us
from broken dreams

Walking down the
middle road to
peace and joy
bright beautiful
salvation

Love Embers

We stand at
the crossroads crying
out fanning the
embers love lost

but not gone
years of lonely

hearts wanting to
hold each other
wishing warm embraces

where love still
lives kindling small
fires knowing that
our love will

burn bright again
we have each
other our passion
will blaze forever

Sun and Shadows

Clouds unite to
send a message
of quiet desperation
but a calming

presence slowing
life down breathing
deeply dancing
down the path

of no return
but wait now
I see sun
shyly shining

through the melancholy
felt by my
lonely heart beating
the drums of

smiling sun
lonely love
walking the
middle road

Lost Lives

Street people
wandering lonely
lost lives
sad souls

moving corner
to corner
one step
ahead of

police their
crimes being
lost living
hand to

mouth I
hope that
they will
come in

Out of the Shadows

Dark street
holding
back bonfires
I

squint against
the
headlights glare
sirens

shreek their
vile
songs it
shakes

my jangled
nerves
my heart
hammers
against

fear
strikes out
silent
screams

Rain

The rain washes
the delicate flower
I cry at
the simple beauty

of hummingbirds flailing
and drinking flowers
sweet food it
is one moment
of pure joy

A Thin Wall

Holed up in
a cheap hotel
a room where
noise sneaks through

A thin wall
he wonders what
landed him there
among the whores

junkies lonely lives
losers running
out of options
he is hiding

from himself the
mess he has
made a perfect
life shattered like

glass hitting bricks
he loads the
gun unable to
shoot his
way toward peace
instead he waits
to be saved
from his nightmare

Words

Words
wailing like
sirens
deafening roar

tell me
a
story don't
leave

anything out
hiding
out in
my

empty space
rocking
my heart
asleep

Riding the Wave

Surfing sadness
unspeakable joy
lying in
bed black

dreams dark
night sun
bright I
want to

find a
happy medium
between manic
ecstasy and

psychotic pain
looking for
balance on
a tightrope

Love Twice

I went to
the beach
and watched the
sand being drawn

into the raging
sea like my
phantom love
blowing into wind

ghost not something
to hold on
to but the
rock stands tall

and splits ocean
into water wings
my love is
strong against

like a deafening
drum
my love

peeks
shyly out
of
the shadows

Change

Frowns into smiles
rain into sun
sorrow into joy
arrogance into humility

dark into light
sadness into hope
death into birth
empty into full

silence into song
fear into peace
war into flowers
I into we

illness into health
sorrow into happiness
chaos into solitude
stagnation into change

Storyteller

I listen for
a story of
love and pain
told by a

person I don't
know or a
family member
and I feel

that I have
been told by
God to tell
stories of

life and death
and everyone
I meet has
a story that

matters and I
try to tell
it with passion
and honest feeling

Sanctuary

Inside the walls
of a hospital
for the mind
I spent time

where others fight
to get out
I find it
to be my

sanctuary and
I make friends
of other people
in their own

crises and we go
home or to
a beautiful
home full of

friendly faces
professional but
warm of heart
and helping

people go back
to their homes
and all the
outpatient nurses

and doctors and
therapists help
to create my
own sanctuary

Starting Over

He walks in
sunlight not
realizing that
light can lead

to a bipolar
black hole
and he wants
to do everything

at once in
a manic movie
and he is
starting over

and the bipolar
blue color
is leading
him down a

path to ruin
and he doesn't
know how to
step carefully

through the minefield
of madness but
maybe the path
leads to a

refuge of
hope and healing
the way to
salvation is

to stop and
let his mind
slow and face
the unseen fear

First Love

My first love
was a temptress
seductive yet
satanic and I

lusted after her
with an obsession
that bordered on
insanity and I

lived with another
woman but my
first love was
always in the

forefront holding
me in her
sharp claws
and I would

do anything go
anywhere to
possess her
poison but the

other woman waited
patiently as I
tried to keep
the temptress

from killing me
and I thought she
would take
me to the

ovens of hell
but the true
love of a
wonderful woman

saved me but
I know that
I can never ignore
the satanic temptress

Boy at the Beach

A boy maybe
five or so
seeing the
wondrous waves

his wide-eyed
awe his first
sight of nature's
breathless beauty

joyful splashing
sea's songbook
waves of wonder
awash in innocence

One Word

one
word
shards
of

sun
piercing
a
frozen

heart
denting
darkness
loving
light
leaning
toward
tomorrow

He
waits
for
love

lingering
in
friendly
fog

Love Embers

We stand at
the cross roads crying
out fanning the
embers love lost

but not gone
years of lonely

hearts wanting to
hold each other
wishing warm embraces
searching silent places

where love still
lives kindling small
fires knowing that
our love will

burn bright again
we have each
other our passion
will blaze forever

No Words

Writing down
love for another
life leaving me
bruised and bipolar

I found love
my manic mind
anchored by a
woman fighting

her own emotions
standing next to
me holding my
heart gently never

breaking it God
has smiled on
tattered flag
I wave it
happiness hoping that
smiling satin skies
will bring me
to summer's song

Begin

I
begin with
one thought one
word looking for
a second calling

out for reinforcement
they come
tumbling out
in a torrent

my soul
sings of people
gone to
a better

world one
person living
a life
alone imprisoned
in her head
in her bed
she longs for

freedom from
fear I paint
her soul
with love

Rain

Rain falls
on dry
ground soaking
animals flowers

Umbrellas thrive
streams rail
hearts break
waves of

melancholy halted
by friends
praying love
helping us

gray gone
we paint
sunshine souls
wet wisdom

Bright Beings

Sunlight shone
on an
empty room
he awakes

to warm
windows before
shadows spread
their wispy

wings bright
brings butterflies
squirrels scampering
to safety

he smiles
at the
simplicity of
it all

Lost and Found

She stands
alone at
the bus
station going

to nowhere
in particular
all the
souls haunt

her she
has lost
her way
looking for

the road
to redemption
she wants
to be
headed toward
the beach
she is
headed nowhere

Soul Searching

Going down a
path filled with
rocks hurting my
feet but I

walk on to
soft dirt soul
searching for the
answer to a

question getting back
to the beginning
you wait wanting
to sleep next

to my touch
my skin smile
at my sleeping
body love lasts

Tunnel

Lights in town
dim as twilight
slips in like
a ghost then

darkness covers the
hills people hiding
from their demons
afraid of black

holes worrying about
being trapped on
a train traveling

to madness through
a tunnel covered
in a black
curtain but then

they see a
small light at
the end urging
them to get
off the train
and closer to
the light hoping
to smile again

Sea of Doubt

Making the maiden
voyage sailing the
melancholy sea of
doubt looking for

a simple sail
warmth of sun
smile lost in
manic madness

anger anxious army
forming for an
attack trying for
the destruction

cities crumbling down
roads muddied by
tears tracing faces
looking upward heaven sent

www.ingramcontent.com/pod-product-compliance
Lightning Source LLC
Chambersburg PA
CBHW030140100526
44592CB00011B/981